Delinquent Palaces

Delinquent Palaces

Danielle Chapman

POEMS

TRIQUARTERLY BOOKS/NORTHWESTERN UNIVERSITY PRESS

EVANSTON, ILLINOIS

TriQuarterly Books
Northwestern University Press
www.nupress.northwestern.edu

Printed in the United States of America

10   9   8   7   6   5   4   3   2   1

Library of Congress Cataloging-in-Publication Data

Chapman, Danielle.
    [Poems. Selections]
    Delinquent palaces : poems / Danielle Chapman.
        pages cm
        ISBN 978-0-8101-3094-4 (pbk. : alk. paper) — ISBN 978-0-8101-3102-6 (ebook)
    I. Title.
    PS3603.H363A6 2015
    811.6—dc23

                                                                    2014046420

The paper used in this publication meets the minimum requirements of the American
National Standard for Information Sciences—Permanence of Paper for Printed Library
Materials, ANSI Z39.48–1992.

For Christian

Elder, Today, a session wiser
And fainter, too, as Wiseness is—

I find myself still softly searching
For my Delinquent Palaces—

—EMILY DICKINSON, POEM 959

CONTENTS

Acknowledgments   *xi*

I

If   *5*
Expressway Song   *6*
Cash Money   *8*
Natural History Museum   *9*
Meet Me in Hollywood   *10*
Epicurean   *11*
Dead Dad Dream   *12*
In Order   *13*
An Autobiography   *14*
The Brighton Basement   *16*
Lower East Side Inventory   *18*
A Premonition   *19*
Silverdale   *20*
Fairfield in August   *22*

II
A Shape Within   *25*

III
Rituxan Spring   *41*
Of Beauties   *42*
Destination Wedding   *44*

Letter from a Small Town   45
Insomniac Country   47
Relapse   49
O Chicago Purgatorio   50
Let Alone   51
View from the Family Room   52
I'd Rather Go with You   53
New Haven   54
Our Bed   55
From Inside   56
Believer   57

ACKNOWLEDGMENTS

Grateful acknowledgment is made to the following publications, in which these poems first appeared:

The Atlantic Monthly: "Believer"

The Chronicle of Higher Education: "Of Beauties"

The Harvard Review: "A Shape Within"

Literary Imagination: "Insomniac Country" and "Lower East Side Inventory"

The Nation: "Destination Wedding" and "Dead Dad Dream" (the latter forthcoming)

New England Review: "In Order"

The New Yorker: "Epicurean"

Poetry International: "An Autobiography," "The Brighton Basement," "O Chicago Purgatorio," and "Rituxan Spring"

Poetry Northwest: "A Premonition" (published as "Afterlife"), "Meet Me in Hollywood," and "Natural History Museum"

Poetry Review (U.K.): "Expressway Song"

TriQuarterly: "If" and "Letter from a Small Town"

Virginia Quarterly Review: "Silverdale"

"In Order" was also featured on Poetry Daily.

Delinquent Palaces

I.

_____

If

I will drive to meet you in the middle
of the night, but if you forget or miss
your plane or if the plane blows up
in the Black Hills and gears go up in smoke
and I become my mother treading water
as my dad goes down, an orphan
in a creek of snakes, if they decide
to gut the creek, to build a freeway through it,
if I become a creature of gasoline and static,
my eyes outdone, men plowing past
in 18-wheelers, night chopped up in crystal
syllables, road blasted to ecstasies
of concrete, some resembling God,
others you, don't ask what I will choose.

Expressway Song

The expressway encircled me
and this was why I'd come: to love,
believing in a love like work,
knowing the true work is waking
to pierce each morning with intent
and evening with irreverence
until the city surrenders,
lifts its iron, and lets one in
with the grace of a raising bridge.

This was why I'd hung my hurts
the way dogs hang their heads out cars,
grinning at oncoming air
as if all experience were fresh
despite the concrete evidence,
the bitter dust that flies through fur
from strips of planted juniper
behind which new construction lies
next to the gutted corner stores.

Why I left, knowing who I was
no more than I had at seventeen,
driving the same piece of junk
that hauled me up the Turnpike then,
low on oil and antifreeze,
speeding through Chicago's sprawl
as I had New Jersey's reeds,
its boxcars and refineries,
sucking in the building buzz—

I drove until it looked like home,
till all the houses were the same,
azaleas clumped around the decks,
men in short sleeves tending them,
and I pulled into a cul-de-sac
to listen to the honeyed talk
of a family by a man-made lake,
watching oak fuzz fall like worms
to water warmer than a womb.

When it was dark and they were gone,
I drove back the way I'd come
and exiting the tunnel where
the expressway throws her hair
in snakes over the stadium
and the architecture vies to be
most dire and most angular,
a voice fell through me like cold chrome—
we come to love what turns to stone.

Cash Money

To love you is to love the grackles screaming
in Starbucks' single tree
as dove hunters unpile trucks
in the season's fluorescent pink fatigues,

to build a teensy fortress of Dante's hell
within the real one, to read
while the underworld takes
Texas back again.

Just married we drove the shorn brown hills
toward the state hospital at Vernon,
cows drinking at lakes' dulled steel
while your eyes roared blue over fields of cotton

to your father's house, an excuse so far
from his first it was almost invisible, almost
impossible, the glass table he handed the bills across
a mirage at marriage's edge—

This never happened, he said,
while outside white concrete smarted
with sun relentlessly promising
us everything.

Natural History Museum

for Kate

Jets still whistle, flags still wag
their tongues, the rhetoric over Washington
still sounds like toothpicks falling
to the linoleum of a million
prefabricated homes, and we glide
through the Smithsonian like piquant teens
coming out of a first foreign language film,
erotic subplots in us now like prehistoric squids;
we blaze through leopardine chimeras,
glaze-streaked Chinese tombs,
rats roasting under a sky that moans
an elephant's lopsided worksong,
comparing each other's eyes to gemstones
scarred with malachite. *We pawned them*, we say,
and got them back from the voodoo market—
there they'd sat beside the tiger claws
in that ancient auditorium of spice.
We guessed this war before it came. We sucked
on stinging nettles. We uglied jungles.
We watched brains grilled at the bazaar.

Meet Me in Hollywood

I let myself go and watched the signs arriving green
in the violet glow Los Angeles put out over the freeway
through the boulevards and bad apartments
to that pink Best Western tangled in the hills
where he stood smoking by the windowsill,
the hot day hung behind him like an outfit bought on debt,
the little fuchsia exhalations of the bougainvillea sexual
and suicidal.
                We drove to Malibu, speeding through
billboards, oil fields, mechanical beaks pecking the soil
till wildflowers sparked the cliffs and our wish
for love mounted the coast like an infatuated angel
evening drowned with its appetite for alcohol
and argument while a mural of Clint Eastwood
smirked over the motel pool.
                                Late that night,
someone walked gently in the room, then left as in a dream
and, switching on the lamp, we found my purse was gone,
a handyman trembling with it in the rhododendrons.
He handed it back as if he'd expected to be caught,
or we'd requested something to be stolen.

Epicurean

On mosaic-tiled abalone stairs
the mayor one-upped a local genius
with one about a wolverine
who swam down from Eau Claire
for weasel season in the Chicago River.
All the pricklefeather ladies wore
coyote skulls instead of hats
to high tea at the Peninsula,
and a foam chest arrived at the door—
four flavors of cream and one blood-orange
sorbet in dry ice from Nairobi.
A forty-dollar tangerine of nutmeat
ribboned by slender Greek
fingers of lovers so charmed
his coiffed stubble matched her armpit hairs
was handed to me, apotropaically,
while every day I remembered reading
Middlemarch outside the zoo,
riding my bike into the Air & Water Show,
fuming at Bellow as the bombers tore
repellently close to the Hancock Tower,
pedalling away from Ashkenazi
with your smile slicing through me
ruthlessly as Rufus slamming the blade
through blush pastrami—Oh!
Intensity! What am I to do with you, I
whose only dream was to inspire
the celebrity chefs at war
to make with liquid nitrogen
what Murano glassblowers did with fire?

Dead Dad Dream

That shape against the morning
like the scalded moon above a canyon,
fine, close-shaven hair as raven
as some fainting maiden's in an opium lair,
or a bear's, or a mink's on the frontier
before it stank of gunpowder,
jaw sharp as a shark's though handsome
as the hum of tractor-trailer brakes
unfailing in the desert, never searing
prickly pear nor even tearing off
a single salmon stem, one hand on
the double pram, rocking grandchildren
while the horizon pinked with sands sinks
into his skin, as if it were the land.

In Order

I've filled my lungs with fog.
I have sobbed in certain, familiar attics
where each fond object had been
hung or shoved away by hands
whose roughness I had loved,
and the carpet smelled of beloved dogs.

Now that that grief's gone and others come
I come back again to understand
the first one, plum blossoms brushing
the attic window as I look out upon
a yard that has been left untended
by any hand but that of God.

An Autobiography

Russia was a stupid country, wasn't any work
to do, we lay around all day gobbling novels.
Father'd bring each of us a book
from Petersburg, sometimes bound in leather,
the pages edged in gold. But when he got old
he couldn't remember a thing, not even
our names. He'd sit all day in his chair
and when he wanted something he'd yell, "Walter!"
and we all skittered, none of us of course
a Walter. Your father's sisters barked
he'd gone berserk marrying an ox like me.
They fawned on him because of that matinee-
star hair; they didn't know nothing
about men who like being bossed. I was boss
of the whole crew, so I could sneak off
and pick the berries straight into my mouth.
I'd never seen fruit like in the Fraser Valley—
Baby Blues ten times as fat as Johnny Trapp's.
But I hope to God you never have to see a hop,
furry little green pinecones that black your hands
like an African's, and nothing gets it off
but hop juice itself. You know the Lord appeared
to me in the hop fields once. *You should be ashamed!*
Hilda yipped, in a snit again about the sin of beer.
I tell you, I turned and He was there: The Lord
at the next braid of hops. He didn't look, just kept on
pulling down garlands. The dew fell, splashing
His eyelashes, but He didn't wipe the water off,
just kept working hop cones off the branch, tossing
them into the barrel between us. When I looked in
it was full of hops, wet and spongy yet suddenly
I could see the pollen packed in every bell,

the petals trembling fair as a child's arm hairs
when it gets the chill, each so fragile, so eager
I wept for having treated them so rough.
But I can't say the hunger left me right away.
Just after, I had an urge to find a blackberry
bramble and smash a bunch against my tongue
just to prove I was still Betty Klassen.
Must've been Old Horny making his last stand
because ever since I've praised Christ for every taste
of His abundance. If Canada's like this, dear,
can you imagine the fruit that waits for us in Heaven?

The Brighton Basement

Our revels now are ended.
—PROSPERO

Beehived birds in thigh-high boots
drained the dregs of Moscow Mules
and from the sea of trouser suits
a bloke shouted, *We fancy you.*

We're in a band called Luxury, he said
with my best mate Ollie.
You're from New York? My God.
Isn't it violent? Like in Menace II Society?

I laughed and slipped off to the loo
where a kohl-eyed local roared
Mind your elbow you bloody whore
and cut me in the queue.

The DJ put on "Sex Machine."
Last orders please! the barman called.
A number for the sexual assault hotline
was scrawled in marker on the stall.

When I returned the bloke declared
The German birds are having a thing.
Let's go, he said, then snogged me hard
against the bar's wood paneling.

The lights came on, I went along
with mods (or rockers?) in the glow
of the palace's ornamental onions
to a house just off the Grand Avenue

where ransacked rooms opaque with smoke
revealed pissed beauties staring out
of ink-black mullets and mohawks
from heaps of Jackie-O coats.

Morning came, we strolled downhill
beside graduated beds of shrubs
where we spotted a bit of foil:
Oxo! he shouted; I replied, *bouillon cube.*

At the beach a metal sheet of holes
formed a profile of two girls kissing
which changed, depending on the angle,
to two boys, then one apiece—

*Mental, innit ? Some clever Sussex lad
built that.* The Channel, pixilated, swelled.
My boot heels sank in shells, not sand.
In Brighton, yeah, we call 'em shingles.

A ruined dock crept out from shore,
a weather-battered cake on stilts,
a sight it seemed I'd seen before.
The old West Pier, he said. *They'll sell it*

For ten quid if you promise to restore it.
Gazing out at that ornate disaster
it seemed that I could hear the moment
at the moment it was outlasted.

Lower East Side Inventory

The gong over Houston (which was the sun)
has rung. Late news: a monsoon,
children up to their necks
in Bronxsville. The view:
Midtown's futurist harmonicas.

Jo Kim's dad is dead next door.
A cop takes notes on a Lilliputian pad,
another wheels him out in black
plastic through halls insulting
themselves with Ajax.

Downstairs, hipsters spill up electric
poles, chewing gum aggressively
and Pedro belts *if I were a rich man,*
rich man, la-da-da-da-da, I'd get
another hooker every night.

O gutter-red sunset seeping
into every crack of silhouette Manhattan
like a teabag steeping through the dark,
come down on Rivington, Chrystie,
Roosevelt Park. Let me sleep.

A Premonition

I went out onto old Orchard:
barred windows lit with immigrants
at dinner, a shadow of pickle carts
and laundry lines between the tenements.
And it was there, among the wares
dragged out by men who stared girls down
like ducks under heat lamps in Chinatown,
barking, *Lady, get your leather here*
that an idea planted itself in the street
and mushroomed obscenely over
the Historic Bargain District—
slamming every shop gate shut,
darkening the facades like a pass
before hard rain, swinging the dimmed
shop signs on their chains so it seemed
the city might bloom black and retreat
into the silhouette of terror at its core,
the world returned to what it was
before us, save for the indestructible bits
of trash blown across the fuming grids
where we'd lived.
                                Yet the next morning
I was left, and the trains kept running.
Pigeons flung themselves from the rails
toward dials of melted snow,
steam columns rose from the roofs
of high buildings, latticed white
with reflection, and the sun
lay a lace of frost and salt
over the pavement and the bridges
while the voice within the light
all but voiced, *this is enough.*

Silverdale

I. Koi

Within the hush of birch medallions,
fir fingers, wild scallions—
that company of dancers held
in a spell of postures before breeze—

Beneath the Mennonite quilt
of cabbages, sugar peas, raspberries,
greenhouse grapes and lettuces,
embellishment of rose trellises—

In the Japanese garden sunken
like a jewel, they swirled in a pool
lipped with shells of pearl and amethyst,
morose as mandarin ghosts—

Eyes bulging at the ends of tangerine
hammerheads backed in golden foil,
tails swishing slow as harem fans
through someone else's Eden.

II. Virgin Forest

Resisting the pull of earth, the cedars' breath
        soured by carcasses; steeled
by pools in alder where bears and cougars drank;

so as not to become too elfin, not to succumb
        to flowers of ground-rot, nor hear
the floor jitter its armor of millipedes

and maggots warring to devour pelts; nor err
        on the side of svelte toadstools,
white helmets drawn down in mounds of mold;

or think the weird tune of fungus (silent, fibrous
        footprints) lovelier than trumpets
of ferns selected by a shaft of sun as one

imagines the elect suddenly stunned in cathedrals,
        spines arched to collect and spill
illumination back into themselves,
                                  she went in.

Fairfield in August

Daylight delivers the althea's twisted rags
and mimosa shag to fire, a scythe edge takes
a pair of tanned old legs out of the hedge,
the bright boredom of corn maddens
with the sound of its own rustling,
and bloodroot rages through the delicate
Queen Anne's lace in pastures blazing
with the silence of summers already spent.

But afternoon still fools us into indolence:
nothing to do but wait for cocktail hour
when cool air blows up from the river,
June bugs gleam, weevils spool
into dustholes, screendoors clap in frames
and names take their chairs among the stars.

II

———

A Shape Within

Not for this were my wings fitted: save only
that my mind was smitten by a lightning flash
wherein came to it its desire.

—*PARADISO* XXXIII, 139, DANTE

The memory of my early pursuit of enigmas, in the time of my
discovery of life and of poetry, returns to my mind. Annoyed, I banish
the thought at once. "I am not tempted (I lie) by the impossible as I
was formerly. I have seen too much suffering (how indecent)." And
her answer: "To believe anew will not increase the suffering. Be open."

—"MAGDALENE WAITING," BY RENÉ CHAR,

TRANS. WILLIAM CARLOS WILLIAMS

1. St. Brigid's

The truck turned, and he stood under the trees
in a Newport shirt and dungarees,
the breeze knocking petals down around him,
stilling the sun in a spray so I could see
each circuit of caught fire pause
before it fell to the chartreuse
oak fuzz already fallen to the ground
and he came through that haze, though as he passed
Our Lady of His Charity, a superstition
seemed to flit across his brow;
he crossed himself and then, as I'd once seen
an unrepentant temptress strut
from a confessional in Italy,
his lips his fingers touched and slow, slow,
he leaned toward the church and lifted
his eyes to me—*O Lord, tangled up in misery.*

2. Afterward

I stood at the library window scared
by how remote the couples shuffling through
spring's phosphorescent greens appeared.
I was alone, but my bones glowed like radium,
my veins cerulean ink blown through glass.
I was a mystical cadaver, a lapse in frequency,
a tear across time, transparent, lit,
imperiled by texture, without even the stain
of bitter plum to lick off my lips.

What was I seeing, how was I being known?
Not by him, but by a brash wind blowing—
toward what?

            I soared above Broadway, a being
made of magazines, glossed down to the core,
lifted by the billboards' deities
bestowing their minuscule papal smiles.
How could I break into the corner store
and tell the customers this news
that had no words, just a register, a radiance
that bolted through every face, rendering each
adorable, and lost?

3. Grand Street

Chinatown flashed like a brain in creation:
chrome frying cages, rotisseries for sale,
fluorescent egg-glazed mung-bean buns,
silver scales brandishing smelts' silver scales,
trim businesspeople in razored suits
inspecting growths on bulbous vegetables,
laborers stippled pale with drywall chalk
darting out of the subway tunnels,
and the tiny sages in oily rags
hobbling through the alley villages—
the light judged each integral to all.

4. 94 Rivington

The light was changed, my belongings strange
as if my life there had already passed:
the kettle stood dutiful in its steam ghost,
green as an aquarium in the algal glow
of the window washed in pigeon guano.
An envelope announced itself
from a pile—those numerals, that name
wrought out of randomness into time.
Pigeons roosting in the trash chute cooed,
then, as one, crashed to the square of sky above.

5. Illumined

At five the windowsill still lolled in sun.
I lay in bed cloaked by a light that cloyed
like unction for an invalid, nauseated
by the idea of a love no tongue could taste,
jailed in an illumined honeycomb.
I dropped a white wad of gum into a glass
of ginger ale. Bubbles rose like souls
unburdening from selves, bearing tiny spheres
of bliss that broke upon the surface
like sleepers to the touch of consciousness.

6. Fire

The word *beautiful* broke in my ear
and remained in the air like a kiss on the skin
after waking from the dream of it, in the green
glow of the bodega and the chattering
parrot kept by the unshaven men
arguing in Spanish, cutting evening open
with its dumb nub of tongue, guttural
in summer air where toddlers bounced to the bass
of passing Jeeps and whores circled like bream
scattering glitter when cop cars came.
I swooned through neon till concrete colors
seared molten, the yellow of curbs multiplied
to dying stars, the fire hydrants redder
than berries of blood on islands of thorn.

7. Question-Beast

Hot under the bars' carnelian dark,
hungrier for my loss of appetite,
as if what I had sought now hunted me,
every glint in shop glass asked:

On Houston, the double helix of the ghetto
barber pole twirled upward till it ended
with:

and began again:

Inside the pizza place neon cases hummed
and servers beamed like recent converts
between a stainless oven and hot pies
blistering with cheese, their eyes reflected
in each mirrored wall, each napkin dispenser,
each knife blade another mirror turning
its glare to hiss:

8. Judgment

Flags above the Pitt Street grocery store
grand opening banner ripped
into the bare sky frightfully exultant—
red, blue, yellow, each declaring
victory against the air.

Three Crips flashed across the projects' veldt
spitting apocalyptic raps.

A scenester strutted past,
boom box blasting "Ghetto Superstar."

And among the towers' high barred squares
the stare of a grandmother
magnified my skin's pallor to a flare.

What more can I do? I cried.
The bright sky scathed, *Repent your pride!*

9. East River Park

Escaping through the crashing gates
of other peoples' heavens

>   I silked my knees in brooks of shadows
>   jinxed out of comprehension.

Under the Domino Sugar crown
the river's cashmere roiled

>   and as if blown by a chariot
>   each blade of grass bowed down

>   then recoiled with a sound like nails
>   thrilling through fields of glass.

10. Distress & Dereliction

Why did the skies break in a brittle chorus
when I woke next, tuned in to a frequency
past hearing? Around the oxide turquoise dome
of St. Xavier and Lenin's statue atop Red Square,
through that vast silhouette of air
"Ave Maria" rang in voices solemn,
disembodied, and electric, igniting
the pavement's gray to a defiant white,
the ornate edifices and plate-glass windows
of boutiques and Laundromats on Ludlow
stunned out of their charming grit
by this radiance merciless toward all shadow.

When I walked out onto Orchard Street
that evening, I saw the disaster life
would be if mankind spent its last belief:
Tenements rose in walls on either side—
uninhabited, purposeless gray shells—
and shop signs swung from their long chains
in a single motion but without a groan
as if they'd abandoned themselves to a fate
in which nothing would happen again.
The only sound was empty juice jugs butting
gutters, of a wind that condescended
to fill things with a brief whistling that moved
through them but delivered them nowhere.
There was no love here. There never had been.
The light had been my imagination.

11. Chimera

He was there
          just where he'd said he'd be

Under the scaffolding on Stanton, the felon
within the image by St. Brigid's:
                      Paradise
collapsed into one face, one hand
reaching into his pocket for a perfect white
packet of oblivion.
            He stepped off the curb.
Asphalt sank beneath his feet:
                  as if the street
were an organ of pedals tarred together
sound and matter flowed
from each footprint in a wave   that as it hit

the limit of my seeing   seizured

four chords
        that halted in a breakbeat—
                    Christ,
what I'd have sold to do that with my voice.

What lips what fingers touched
my face   (what bliss,
                  what humiliation)
      before the block sucked him back—

      See you round, I guess

and I was left   with my creation?

12. Mercy

The hall went dark as before a summer storm
and as if I'd breathed a rag of fine black lace
doused in chloroform or kissed an incubus
I choked upon the stink of my extinguishment,
ammoniac upon the street's corruption.
Make me pure, I whispered, and a vision appeared:

Mary, medieval and weird, opening like an iris,
each hand a slip of glycerin, her bodice intricately
brailled with pain, quivering in the acrid air,
a cool blue shape within that burn
that left its stain on the apartment's atmosphere
that I might remember no one once loved me there.

Coda

Beyond the speeches we're given to when young—
the crystal moon, the harlot moon, the moon
big as the sun elongating scrolls
of banisters on the skin of someone
else so young—beyond the still moon cut
from a royal purple sky we stare into
as into the pupil of a beautiful
machine—beyond our grand stupidities—
the urgency won't perish: to be known
in one's own person as crocuses are known
by sun, conceiving green to breathe it,
for ravishment by light, to grow
into the moment in our cells when we open
ourselves as a plant uncoils pistils
and become refulgent whether looked at or not.

III

Rituxan Spring

Known as a "chimeric antibody," Rituxan
is a drug made of tissues from two species

As derricks draw ink
from parched plains
we've struck

Time, silky and game
as a stick streaming
snake roe.

This must be a dream—

spring singing slime
through snail stones,

membranous hollows
trembling tadpoles'
fatigue greens,

truffle caps fretted
as girdles of whalebone,

musk like the civet's
resurrected in cologne.

Love, let me kiss
the rodent
who died for this.

Of Beauties

for E. & F.

Oh child

Out of the scorch
of oil fields
and cliffs of cotton felled
to radiant Tarnation

From coral foxholes
splintering shrapnel
to Oriental jungles

Through interstices of pain
where God's green
meets man's limestone

You come, little ones

As unknown
to the heat-crazed grasses
white obelisks stab at

As to undreamed rimed streets
parboiled with pitbulls

You come

Through the commute's
python inching
to strangle

the skyline's
indigestible jewel

Into the balconies' twinkle,
the yawn of wharves,
the channel between
blacked galleries dwarfed
by the El
and vertical blue
precipitous coves

You cartwheel
to the core
of the city
of the year
of innocence

Where windows dwell
on the silenced
stage-lit séance
of angular furniture
and the hospital
garage crooners recall
every floor

You
murmur rapture

Life
out of nothingness

Mother of beauties
you come through me

Unto us

Twice

Destination Wedding

Drunk as a persimmon
on the wine of Cana or myself I couldn't tell—
the old pain and the old dream mingled
and seasickness threw kisses
in shapes upon the wall like shells
upon the shore outside the conch-
shaped hall in whose pearled hum I danced
as if my feet were small
and free of gravity as sea lice.
When above the palms, horns, drums, and silks
I heard a creature high in moss-
tangled eucalyptus cry for milk—
a creature not my own, yet still
my milk let down.
I looked up and it locked me
in a stare, half child, half marsupial,
that transfixed me on the scallop
of the terraced white hotel it squatted on
until sure that I had seen it
it dove back into the lagoon
like a weasel chasing an eel
ever further into the nature of oblivion.

Letter from a Small Town

Leaves confess their red
and gold to hills
of mud, necks of brutes
cologned with clover.

Rain blears to absinthe
on the windshield,
transparent dots
of green.

Outbursts of desire
come around in carfuls,
brash pansies bloom
out of the bricks.

I should smoke
the pleasure-tickets
that shake out
of summer's pockets,
let some fragrance
cure the glare

but I've always wanted
more, my fond
and bitter rag.

If only I could knit life
like a sweater
and stroll around
in a mood

of such smart refusal
that everyone would spit
or fall for it

but none would dare
ask to see the tag.

Insomniac Country

1. Capitol Reef

Waking into pastel deserts
the soul roams
over cracked blisters
on these wastes of moon

though it also lingers
with the breath
of burros on brief grasslands
islanded in stone

among tiny towns wedged
between slagheaps of granite
like outpourings
of ancient punishment

for those who wake again
to these vast plains
in shanties cowered
by shale chimneys

where two hundred million
years of sediment sleep
soundly through the pain
of consciousness.

2. "Extreme Adventure," 3 A.M. (PST)

The cataract of a dream
shattered into stasis: a planet

of scorpions in distances
of heat so furious

he had to piss on his shirt
and wear it as a turban

so as to not incinerate
his brain. Was it madness

demanded he uncover signs
among those craters

and broke a crack, oracular,
in the desert floor

opening a new ravine within
the heart of this one?

Switchbacks swept back
into a valley of piñon

and misshapen stones
rose like Golgothas

in the falling sun, for once
again it was evening

and again the source
of the dream was gone.

Relapse

How many days did I live
in praise? Two
hundred, three, free
a year from terror.

But now the air's
anguished flavor sweeps
over the glass stairs
in my rearview mirror—

squares deflecting vastness
as the blunt word
tears at my ear
like an axe at the earth.

O Chicago Purgatorio

Are we getting anywhere
in our salted cars,
will the ice melt eat
through sidewalk rinks
left by icicles
freakishly large and aimed
from garage shingles
like an arsenal
of Viking death tools?

Three days in a row
below twenty
below, O Chicago,
Purgatorio, if it's true
that all that gets to you
goes heavenward
why does no
revelation bubble through
December's clear blue
warty swords?

All I hear's the squeal
of Streets and San trucks
spinning wheels
on brined black slicks
and a devil
belching from his hole:
six hundred sixty-six
more weeks of this.

Let Alone

Every spring you yank me back up
to this blossom brink
too bright for any sane comparison—

No person in leaf-flame immolation.

That any two details should gather matter out
of absolute heat!

Let alone on this street.

View from the Family Room

Transplant Ward, 15th Floor

Where steel rails jut pitiless prows into vertigo—

The gulls, and the sails below,
The girls in gold gladiator sandals,
The strollers with twin bicycle wheels—

That crescent of sand and glowering bangle
of traffic below the Drake—

That quarter-mile of hotel, hospital, and lake

My eyes still seek as they fall through
onyx kidneys by van der Rohe—

Where, where, where did it go?

I'd Rather Go with You

I'd rather go with you and mince precisely
through whoop-cream worlds
sugar-belled by kissy-buds
down aisles brailled with frippery—

Let's go galloping, Lieblings,
with the nimbleness of minks across
our circumstance of ice

And like old hippies skinny-dipping
up past the beaver dam
where we honeymooned
back when autumn hydrangeas greened,
never speak of slipping.

In the Chinatown of childhood
a ten-foot-tall deal dresser's hundred drawers
wink open one by one on the miraculous—

We'll make it there, my little livers
and when we do I swear
I shan't be penurious.

New Haven

The fear, admitted, lifted, and my dear
we did it differently, beneath
the rental's pull-chain lanterns
like faintly lit hornet nests,
the one at center a planet of torn paper,
the bed's metal middle foot supported
by a motel Bible
                         as if there could never be
enough
roughness to devour, nor suffering
too great
           for one replete with one
                             and all
the nowheres known together.

Our Bed

I complained it clashed with the easy chair
the boys from Urban Nest convinced us to brocade
in Moorish rosettes, my petty gaze
dumb to its great provender while I labored
miserably to beautify our days. Its grid exposed,
its fake teak slats undone, the headboard's shellacked zen
collapsed, its fat mattress slugged downstairs,
all I wanted from matter was a bit of give—
for you to live. Forever maybe. But tonight,
tossing in this mandarin and white
Alice Washburn in Connecticut all I want
is the seven years that good bed already gave.

From Inside

Sudden geese beyond
the buffered blank that walls us
in, defying all
manner of healing
gardens

Geese
somewhere out there above
the upcupped Bauhaus glass

Honking Bachlike
over the infusion suite
abruptly
lovely, neglectful, no, not
unheedful of the dead

But of the dread
material
in which we wait

Believer

I hadn't wanted to believe myself
numbered among the unlucky ones.
There'd always seemed an arrogance in that
of which my superstition made me wary.
Nor was the title very accurate.
In fact it seemed a blessing or a talent
sometimes, or its own kind of deeper luck,
the way I walked into each suffering
which was its own intricate world complete
with wild children wrangling to be king
of every broken square of concrete
and market stalls of shrimp kept cool on ice
whose infinitesimal limbs caught light
as if hauled glittering into genesis.